A HISTORY OF BRITAIN

Acknowledgments:
The author and publishers would like to thank Mike Gibson for his help in
research, and the following for permission to use illustrative material:
Page 14: Amalgamated Engineering and Electrical Union;
cover: the Bluebell Railway, Uckfield;
pages 23 and 51, and background photograph on pages 2, 3, 50, 51, 54, 55
by Tim Clark; cover and page 16: Co-operative Union, Manchester;
cover and page 33: Courtesy of the Florence Nightingale Museum Trust;
pages 24 and 48: The Illustrated London News Picture Library;
pages 37 and 50: Trustees of the Imperial War Museum, London;
page 23: Courtesy of Mr John Lobley (photograph by Tim Clark);
pages 9, 11, 15 and 46: Mary Evans Picture Library;
pages 22, 29 and 41: Maggie Murray/Format Partners;
page 33 (right): Courtesy of the Director, National Army Museum;
page 27: National Maritime Museum, London;
cover: National Motor Museum, Beaulieu;
page 38: the Robert Opie Collection;
page 7: The Royal Collection © 1993, Her Majesty the Queen;
page 51: the Trustee of the Wellcome Trust.

Ladybird books are widely available, but in case of
difficulty may be ordered by post or telephone from:

Ladybird Books – Cash Sales Department
Littlegate Road Paignton Devon TQ3 3BE
Telephone 01803 554761

A catalogue record for this book is available
from the British Library

Published by Ladybird Books Ltd Loughborough Leicestershire UK
Ladybird Books Inc Auburn Maine 04210 USA

Contents

The Victorians

by TIM WOOD

illustrations by JOHN DILLOW

Series Consultants: School of History
University of Bristol

Ladybird

The Victorian Age

This book covers the 71 years from 1830 to 1901. For most of this period Queen Victoria was on the throne. It was a time of tremendous change in the lives of all Britons.

During this time Britain became the most powerful country in the world with the largest Empire that had ever existed. Britain ruled one fifth of the world's surface and one quarter of the people.

The Victorian Age – people and events

Date	People	Events
1832		The Great Reform Act. It was the first step towards making equal sized voting areas
1834		Slavery abolished in all British Colonies
		Poor Law Amendment Act. Introduced a new and tougher system of poor relief
1835		Town councils were allowed to set up their own police forces
1837		Queen Victoria crowned on the death of William IV
1840		Penny Post introduced
1842		Mines Act ended child and female labour in the coalmines
1845		Irish Potato Famine
1847	James Simpson	The first anaesthetic
		10-Hour Act introduced a maximum 10-hour day for women and young people in cotton factories
1848	Edwin Chadwick	First Public Health Act
1851	Prince Albert	The Great Exhibition

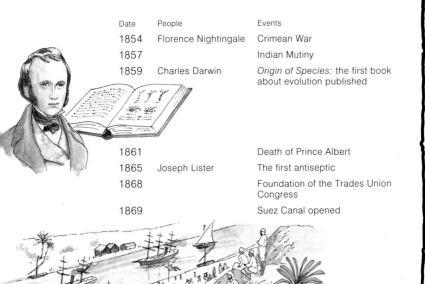

Date	People	Events
1854	Florence Nightingale	Crimean War
1857		Indian Mutiny
1859	Charles Darwin	*Origin of Species:* the first book about evolution published
1861		Death of Prince Albert
1865	Joseph Lister	The first antiseptic
1868		Foundation of the Trades Union Congress
1869		Suez Canal opened

Date	People	Events
1870		The Education Act introduced State Elementary Schools for children aged 5–10
1871		First FA Cup competition
1876		Victoria made Empress of India
1879		Zulu War
1880		First Boer War
	Joseph Swan	First demonstration of electric lighting
		Elementary education made compulsory
1882		Married women allowed to own property for the first time
1883		First Australia v England cricket match for the Ashes
1885		First motor bike
		General Gordon killed at Khartoum
1889		Dockers' Strike
1897		Victoria's Diamond Jubilee
1898		Sudan conquered
1901		Death of Queen Victoria

Victoria and Albert

Princess Victoria was brought up very strictly. She was not allowed to speak to adults unless her governess was present. She could not read a book without permission. After Victoria became Queen at the age of 18, this all changed. She had to talk to the Prime Minister, and to read and sign important state papers.

Victoria inherited the throne from her uncle William IV (1830-1837). He was known as the 'Sailor King' because of his interest in the Royal Navy.

When Princess Victoria became Queen, she reigned longer than any other British monarch. Later in her reign, Victoria became the ruler of many lands as the British Empire grew. She was called Empress of India. Huge crowds celebrated the Golden Jubilee which marked her 50th anniversary as Queen.

The young Queen Victoria and Prince Albert
with five of their children

Three years later, Victoria married a
German prince, Albert. They adored each
other and they had nine children. Albert
became his wife's closest adviser.
When he died after 21 years of
marriage, Victoria went into
mourning for years.
She wore black,
was rarely seen in
public and became
known as the
'Widow of Windsor'.

A pottery figure
of Victoria
produced at the
time of her
coronation

Religion

Christianity had a very important influence on Victorian society. Religion affected every aspect of people's lives. It encouraged many people to provide *charity* at home and be *missionaries* abroad. Churches also provided most of the schools in Victorian England.

Giving charity to less fortunate neighbours became a Christmas custom for the rich

In 1851, the number of people attending church was counted nationally for the first time. About 60% of those over 10 years old attended. This is very high by our standards, but the Victorians thought more should attend.

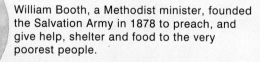

William Booth, a Methodist minister, founded the Salvation Army in 1878 to preach, and give help, shelter and food to the very poorest people.

Christianity also encouraged people to act in certain ways, which have since been called 'Victorian values'. These values included hard work, thrift, and respect for authority inside and outside the home. Children were expected to be seen and not heard. Many people found it hard to live up to those values, so the Victorians are sometimes accused of having had double standards.

A Quaker soup kitchen

Many great Victorians felt it was their duty to help the poor. Dr Barnardo devoted himself to the care of homeless children. His Barnardo's Homes took in, fed, clothed and educated tens of thousands of poor children.

The Poor Law

During Victoria's reign, most poor people were helped by private charity, which was mainly given by the church. For those who could not get such help, a new system of poor relief had been introduced by the government in 1834.

New farming machines, such as this thresher, and more efficient farming methods put many farm workers out of a job.

The new *poor law* was meant to save money and to encourage people to look for work. All those who needed help, such as orphans, the old, the sick and the unemployed, had to go into a workhouse. By the end of Victoria's reign, conditions in the workhouses had improved. But people still hated these grim places.

In the workhouse, conditions were deliberately made harsh so that only those in real need would enter. Families were often split up, with males and females being separated. The inmates received a bare minimum of food and clothing. In return they had to do hard, boring work, and obey strict rules.

The Victorian public were shocked by the descriptions of workhouse life written by Charles Dickens in his book *Oliver Twist*. In this illustration, Oliver is asking for more food.

Conditions in factories

During the 1800s, the *Industrial Revolution* spread throughout Britain. The use of steam-powered machines, especially in the textile industry, led to a huge increase in the number of factories. Many factory workers were children. They worked long hours and were often treated harshly by the *overseers*.

The first factory laws which laid down rules about pay and working conditions were not very effective. Many machines did not have safety guards and accidents were common. There were few factory inspectors to make sure the laws were obeyed. Children continued to work in factories until 1880, when the introduction of *compulsory* schooling for children aged between five and ten helped to end child labour.

Lord Shaftesbury – 'The Children's Friend'. He worked hard to get laws through Parliament to stop young children having to work.

A birth certificate.
These became compulsory in 1836, making it much easier to check if young workers were under age.

Children did many other horrible jobs. Small boys were sent up chimneys to sweep them by hand until a law introduced in 1875 banned this.

A union emblem

Trade Unions

As more people came to work in factories, mills and mines, they began to group together and form *trade unions*. Most *employers* and the Government disliked unions because they forced up wages and encouraged *employees* to protest about their working conditions.

Many early unions met in pubs which came to be named after them.

They discussed sickness benefits, *burial clubs*, pay and hours of work.

Trade unions grew in spite of this opposition. Skilled workers such as engineers and coal miners formed unions which provided benefits for their members such as sickness and unemployment pay. The union movement slowly spread to less skilled workers on the docks and in transport. By the end of Victoria's reign about a quarter of all workers, both men and women, were members of unions.

Women workers outside a match factory in 1888. Public sympathy was aroused when they went on strike. People were shocked to hear of their low wages and dangerous working conditions.

The Co-operative movement

Another way in which the workers tried to help themselves was through the Co-operative movement. This started when 28 weavers opened a grocery store in Toad Lane in the Lancashire mill town of Rochdale in 1844.

The first Co-op shop in Toad Lane, Rochdale

The shop in Rochdale was so successful that similar 'Co-ops' sprang up in other towns. At this time, food was often impure and goods were poor quality. The Co-ops provided good quality food, clothes and goods at reasonable prices. They also gave ordinary people the chance to save.

How the Co-operative worked

1 Each weaver put in one pound to buy oatmeal, sugar, candles and other household goods.

2 These were sold to customers at fair prices. Each customer also received a *dividend* according to how much he or she had bought.

3 At the end of the year the profits were shared out to the dividend-holders. They could either spend their dividends on goods or leave the money in the business as an *investment* on which interest would be paid.

Many factory owners paid their workers with tokens like this. The workers could only spend them in the factory owner's shop, where prices were high and food was often of poor quality.

Cholera

During Victoria's reign the population of Britain grew at a fantastic speed, increasing from 18 million in 1847 to 39 million in 1901. It grew fastest in London and the new industrial towns of South Wales, the Midlands and the North. Many towns grew too fast for proper planning and became overcrowded. With no efficient rubbish collection or sewage disposal, water supplies were often polluted.

'Night soil men' emptied the privies at night

Town *privies* were shared by several families. Many people collected all their water from public water pumps. Pollution seeping into the water supply from nearby privies, dung heaps and rubbish piles caused diseases which spread like wildfire through the overcrowded slums.

This led to epidemics of killer diseases, such as typhoid and cholera, which persuaded the Government to take action by passing laws to improve water supplies, sewage disposal and housing. Sanitary inspectors and medical officers of health were appointed to make sure the laws were obeyed. This led to a great improvement in health and living conditions in towns which was one of the major achievements of the Victorian Age.

Workers building Victorian sewers. Today our health still depends on their huge engineering achievements.

The Chartists

In 1836, only one male in 40 was allowed to vote. Many working class men, especially skilled or educated craftworkers, were angry that they could not vote. They organised a campaign to make Parliament and voting fairer by collecting signatures for a huge petition or charter. They became known as the Chartists after their charter.

The demands of the Chartists

1 All men over 21 to be allowed to vote
2 All voting to be secret
3 All voting areas to be the same size
4 MPs to be paid
5 People to be allowed to become MPs without being landowners
6 A new Parliament to be elected every year

A cartoon of the time showing the Charter being presented to Parliament. The Charter contained 2 million signatures, but many were forged – Queen Victoria's name appeared 15 times!

As the country became richer, people were more interested in their pay packets than the vote, and the movement died out. Even so, by 1918 all the aims of the charter (except the last one) had been achieved. Today everyone over the age of 18 has the vote.

The Chartists ran their own newspapers and held torchlit processions. But Parliament refused to take any notice of their Charter. Chartist leaders were imprisoned and soldiers were sent to deal with trouble spots in the North where Chartists were rioting.

'The Penny Black' stamp – the first stamp. The introduction of the 'Penny Post' in 1840 helped groups like the Chartists to spread their ideas throughout the land.

Schools

During Victoria's reign a system of *elementary education* for all children was developed by the Church. After 1870, the Government, realising that a well-educated workforce was necessary to run the machines and factories of Britain, played an important part in providing the extra money needed to improve education.

Learning the alphabet in Victorian times

Education concentrated on the '3 Rs' – reading, writing and arithmetic. Teachers were paid according to the results of their pupils. Inspectors toured the schools testing children. 'Payment by results' saved the Government money, but it had a harmful effect on education. Pupils were simply drilled to answer the exact questions they would be asked in the test without learning anything else.

Children at an elementary school. Schooling became free in 1891. Then in 1899, the school leaving age was raised to 12.

A B C D E F G H
a b c d e f g h i j k l
1 2 3 4 5 6 7 8 9

Children were taught copperplate writing

Children used chalk and slates for much of their work

An early first-class train

The railways

The success of early railways, such as the line between Liverpool to Manchester, led to a great increase in railway building in Victorian times. Between 1835 and 1865 about 25,000 kilometres of track were built, and over 100 railway companies were created.

Railway travel transformed people's lives. Trains were first designed to carry goods but soon passengers, especially from the working classes, found they could afford to travel by rail. Cheap Day Excursion trains became popular. Seaside resorts, such as

A poster advertising a railway excursion

Railways even changed the time. The need to run the railways on time meant that *local time* was abolished and clocks showed the same time all over the country.

A third-class train in the 1840s. A Railway Act in 1844 forced all railway companies to run at least one cheap train a day which stopped at every station and cost no more than one penny a mile.

Blackpool and Weston-super-Mare, grew rapidly. The railways also provided thousands of new jobs – building locomotives and carriages, running the railways, and repairing the track and rolling stock.

A Victorian station

Steamships

The first wooden steamships were small, and so much space was needed to carry the coal that there was little room for cargo and passengers. After 1843, much larger steamships with iron, and later steel, hulls were built. The invention of screw propellers, steam turbine engines, oil and diesel engines, and the building of coaling stations along the trade routes, made steamships much more efficient.

The *Great Western*, built by Brunel, was powered by two paddle wheels. Her successful crossing of the Atlantic began the first regular steamship service from Britain to America.

After 1870, steamships brought grain from the USA and refrigerated meat from New Zealand and Argentina. This greatly lowered food prices and raised people's living standards. By 1900, half the world's trade was carried in British ships.

The SS *Great Britain*, built by Brunel, was the first steamship with a screw propeller

Isambard Kingdom Brunel, one of the finest engineers and shipbuilders of Victorian times

Tea clippers, such as the *Cutty Sark*, were faster and could carry more cargo than early steamships. Sailing ships were still in use at the end of Victoria's reign.

The Great Exhibition

In 1851, Prince Albert planned a Great
Exhibition to celebrate the achievements of
British and foreign industry. The Exhibition
was housed in a startling new building made
of iron and glass which was put up in Hyde
Park, London.

The Exhibition was opened by Queen Victoria on 1 May 1851. It was a huge success with over 7000 British exhibitors and 6000 from abroad. The Exhibition was visited by over 6 million visitors, many of whom came on special cheap trains.

A souvenir paperweight and a special railway ticket produced for the Great Exhibition

The Great Exhibition showed the strength of British industry. For the next 20 years Britain was known as the 'workshop of the world'. During the 26 weeks of the Exhibition the visitors ate 2 million buns and drank 1 million bottles of mineral water.

The Exhibition building was nicknamed the Crystal Palace. It was built from 250,000 square metres of glass, 2300 iron girders and 3300 iron pillars which were brought to Hyde Park and then fitted together. It was destroyed by fire in 1936.

Gladstone turned down a career in the Church to go into politics. He had a strong sense of right and wrong and believed people should be judged on their merits, not on their wealth. He supported the right of small nations, including Ireland, to govern themselves.

Gladstone and Disraeli

William Gladstone and Benjamin Disraeli were the two most famous Prime Ministers in Victorian England. Gladstone was the leader of the Liberal Party and Disraeli was the leader of the Conservative Party.

They were both brilliant speakers who could inspire their audiences and they were both great *reformers*. But these two great statesmen had very different ideas and they detested each other. They became great rivals who dominated Victorian politics for nearly 50 years.

The witty Disraeli was an author as well as a politician. He wore fancy clothes and loved to poke fun at the serious-minded Gladstone. Disraeli was a strong supporter of the British Empire. He bought control of the Suez Canal and made Queen Victoria Empress of India.

At election time, both party leaders travelled round the country drumming up support. Gladstone could deliver a speech to thousands of people in the open air with his great booming voice.

The Crimean War

In 1854, Britain and France went to war in the Crimea to support Turkey against Russia. The war was badly organised. The British soldiers were poorly equipped, and before long, cholera and dysentery were sweeping through their ranks.

The Charge of the Light Brigade was one of the biggest disasters of the war. Out of the 673 men who made the charge, only 50 stayed in their saddles, 113 were killed, and many more were wounded or captured – all the result of a mix-up in orders.

Florence Nightingale was sent to the Crimea with 38 nurses. She organised the cleaning of the filthy, rat-infested military hospital at Scutari and organised proper nursing. The death rate fell dramatically. Her remarkable efforts won her the gratitude of thousands of sick and dying soldiers. Nursing became a respectable profession for women as a result of her work.

Florence Nightingale was called 'the lady with the lamp' because every night she toured the wards comforting the soldiers.

Florence Nightingale's lamp looked like this

A brooch presented to Florence Nightingale by Queen Victoria

The Indian Mutiny

In 1857, British rule in India was threatened by a *mutiny* of the *sepoys* in the army of the *East India Company*. This sparked off a great rebellion which swept through much of India. There was savage fighting by both sides before British rule was restored.

The mutiny began when sepoys refused to use cartridges which had been greased with beef and pork fat. Because of their religious beliefs, Hindus refused to touch beef and Muslims refused to touch pork.

After the mutiny Victoria became Empress of India and the country was put under the direct rule of a British *Viceroy*. The Indian princes gave their loyalty to the Crown.

Under the rule of the *Raj*, roads, railways, telegraph and postal services were set up to modernise the country. In return India provided a market for British goods and a supply of men for British colonial armies. India became known as the 'Jewel in the Crown' of Queen Victoria.

A medallion celebrating Queen Victoria as Empress of India

Many Indians, both rich and poor, resented British rule which they felt threatened their traditional way of life. This boiled over into savage fighting during the Indian Mutiny. Both sides behaved with great cruelty.

The Zulu War

Winning an Empire could only be achieved by fighting. British soldiers were fighting a war somewhere in the vast British Empire during every single year of Queen Victoria's reign. One of the fiercest struggles was against the Zulus who threatened British settlers in South Africa.

In January 1879, a British army invaded Zululand. Part of the army was attacked by over 20,000 Zulus at Isandhlwana. The British force of 1500 men, scattered and short of ammunition, was massacred.

Shortly after the disaster at Isandhlwana fewer than 200 British soldiers – many of them wounded – held off a force of 4000 Zulus which attacked them at a mission hospital at Rorke's Drift. The British fired over 20,000 bullets during the battle. After it, 11 Victoria Crosses were awarded – the highest number ever given in a single battle.

ammunition pouch

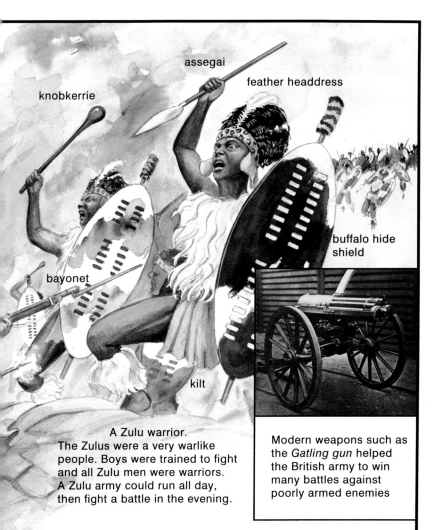

knobkerrie

assegai

feather headdress

buffalo hide shield

bayonet

kilt

A Zulu warrior.
The Zulus were a very warlike
people. Boys were trained to fight
and all Zulu men were warriors.
A Zulu army could run all day,
then fight a battle in the evening.

Modern weapons such as
the *Gatling gun* helped
the British army to win
many battles against
poorly armed enemies

But in the end the Zulus could not win
against modern weapons. In July 1879, the
British army destroyed Ulundi the Zulu
capital. *Cetewayo*, the Zulu king, was
captured and the power of the Zulu army
was broken.

What people ate

Before 1850, surveys showed that up to one-third of people living in cities were extremely poor. Their diet was made up mainly of bread and dripping. After 1850, diet slowly improved as wages rose and cheaper food, such as wheat and meat, came from abroad.

Stores such as Sainsbury, Boots, Marks and Spencer and Woolworth appeared

Some of the packets of food sold in 1880

The quality of food also improved as the food industry went through its own industrial revolution. Factories turned out mass-produced bread, jam, margarine, biscuits, sweets and many other types of food. The growth of the railways and the invention of refrigeration meant that food sold in shops was fresher. The invention of canning helped to bring a more varied diet.

During the 1800s, many famous modern brand names appeared and food advertising began. Advertisements often tried to show the benefits to be gained by eating the food.

Cadbury's cocoa
Makes strong men Stronger!

In rich houses a small army of cooks and servants prepared huge amounts of food. Breakfast alone could include ham, tongue, cold pheasant, partridge, pressed beef, eggs, bacon, kidneys, toast, porridge, Indian and China tea.

Homes

Most poor people lived in terraced houses
near the factory where they worked. Many of
these houses were cheaply and badly built.
They soon became slums. People lived
there in cramped and filthy conditions,
unable to keep their houses clean as
they rotted about them.

Slum housing

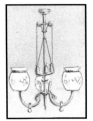

By 1900, most
richer families
had gas lights
like this, or even
electric light

bedroom

drawing
room

A Victorian Villa

decorative stained glass door

The kitchen range heated
the house and the water

kitchen

Middle class people moved out of the dirty inner cities to new, cleaner *suburbs*. The houses here were large and strongly built. The Victorians loved decorations and filled their houses with them.

Some houses had running water and proper bathrooms by 1900. In most houses the water for washing had to be carried upstairs in jugs. People washed in basins on wash stands like this. ▼

housemaid

dining room

scullery

cook

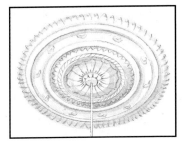

decorative plaster mouldings on ceilings

The Victorians filled their rooms with furniture, paintings and ornaments

Victorian writers

Many famous writers lived in Victorian times. Their novels tell us a great deal about people at the time, and some of the best and worst things about Victorian Britain.

Many of the writers were women, but because books written by women stood little chance of being published, female authors often took male pen names.

Mary Ann Evans wrote her novels under the name George Eliot

The Brontë sisters – Anne, Charlotte and Emily – lived with their clergyman father on the wild Haworth Moors in Yorkshire. It was here that Charlotte wrote *Jane Eyre* and Emily wrote *Wuthering Heights*, both marvellous love stories.

Lewis Carroll was the writer of *Alice in Wonderland*

The greatest Victorian novelist was Charles Dickens. He was a brilliant story teller whose books include thieves, convicts and schoolboys. He wrote about ordinary people and how they lived, about terrible prisons, bad schools and the workhouse. Characters such as Scrooge, Oliver Twist and David Copperfield are known all over the world.

One man whose book became a bestseller was the missionary explorer, David Livingstone. He wrote the story of his amazing three-year journey across the African continent from the Atlantic to the Indian Ocean. He was the first European to see the majestic Victoria Falls.

What people wore

During the first 40 years of Victoria's reign, women wore huge skirts and many petticoats. These layers were supported by a stiff wire cage called a crinoline. Men dressed very plainly in frock coats, waistcoats and trousers.

A woman about 1855

lace cap

lace collar

jacket with slit sleeves

cotton skirt

corset

side whiskers

stiff collar

starched cravat

Poor people often bought second-hand clothes

scarf instead of tie

underfoot straps

A gentleman about 1850

boots

no shoes

A crinoline

Victorian women wore strong corsets stiffened with whalebone or steel. These were laced very tightly to give them tiny waists. Corsets were very unhealthy because they stopped the wearer breathing properly.

By the end of the century many more people could afford to buy fashionable, ready-made clothes from the new department stores.

Women's skirts became much tighter and bell-shaped. Baggy trousers, called bloomers after their inventor, Miss Amelia Bloomer, became fashionable as women's sportswear.

A man about 1900

top hat

starched, stiff collar

waistcoat

frock coat

A woman about 1900

short fitted jacket with puffed sleeves

small 'chatelaine' bag

bell-shaped skirt

tiny lead weights sewn into the hem

high buttoned boots

A woman in formal evening dress about 1870. She is wearing a padded undergarment, called a bustle, which became popular for a brief time.

Sport and leisure

Sport became very popular in Victorian times. Traditional sports, such as football, cricket and boxing, had proper rules for the first time. New sports, such as tennis and rugby, developed.

Dr W. G. Grace, one of England's most famous cricketers, who founded the Gloucester county XI in 1870

Football clubs such as Everton and Aston Villa were set up by churches to attract larger congregations. Others, such as Arsenal, were set up by employers to improve industrial relations. Football was meant to keep people healthy and to encourage a sense of fair play. It wasn't very successful. Free kicks (1877) and penalty kicks (1891) had to be introduced to stop foul play.

The music hall was one of the most popular forms of entertainment for rich and poor who enjoyed the acrobats, magicians, singers and dancers who performed there.

Until the middle of the century most people worked six days a week. The phrase 'the weekend' was not used until about 1870. After the spread of the railways, trips to the seaside and into the country became popular. Those who could not afford to go elsewhere visited their local parks and zoos. Towns began to compete with one another to provide bigger and better tourist attractions.

A big change in Victorian times was that it became respectable for women to play sports

The Diamond Jubilee—the Queen leaving Buckingham Palace

The end of the Victorian Age

In 1897, a Diamond Jubilee was held to celebrate Queen Victoria's 60th year on the throne. Representatives came from all over the Empire to pay their respects. The celebrations and processions were magnificent.

Postage stamps
of the Empire

But the Queen's health was already failing. She spent much of her time in a wheelchair. During the last four years of her reign, she became increasingly ill and depressed.

Queen Victoria at the end of her reign. After her husband's death she was rarely seen in public.

She died on 22 January 1901. All over Britain people went into mourning. Thousands of people went to her funeral. Many wept in the streets as her coffin passed. She was buried beside her beloved Albert, the man she had loved and mourned so long. Her death marked the end of the greatest age in British history.

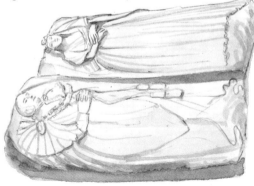

The tomb of Victoria and Albert at Frogmore

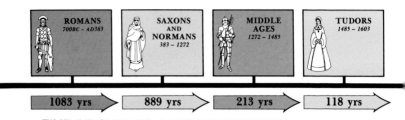

ROMANS 700BC – AD383	SAXONS AND NORMANS 383 – 1272	MIDDLE AGES 1272 – 1485	TUDORS 1485 – 1603
1083 yrs	889 yrs	213 yrs	118 yrs

TIMELINE GUIDE TO *A HISTORY OF BRITAIN*

How we know

The events in this book happened over 90 years ago – so how do we know about them?

Historians use EVIDENCE, rather like detectives do, to piece a story together. There is a huge amount of evidence from this period which has survived.

Photography was invented during the Victorian period. There are many PHOTOGRAPHS and even some FILMS which were taken at the time and show the events as they actually happened.

The first photographs of a foreign war were taken in the Crimea. Some of the scenes they showed shocked many people.

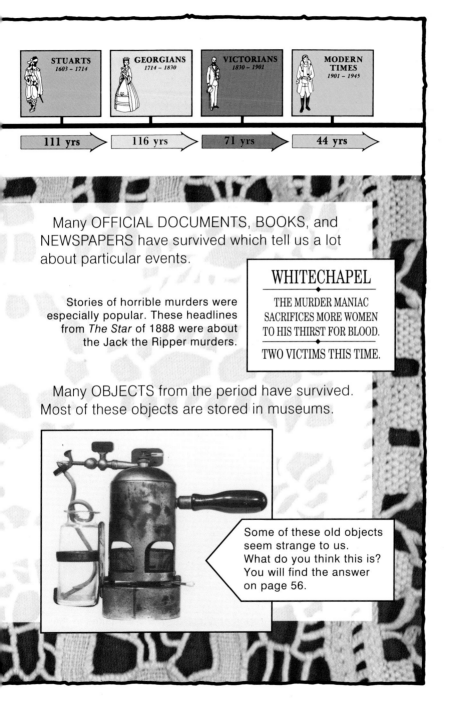

| STUARTS 1603 – 1714 | GEORGIANS 1714 – 1830 | VICTORIANS 1830 – 1901 | MODERN TIMES 1901 – 1945 |

| 111 yrs | 116 yrs | 71 yrs | 44 yrs |

Many OFFICIAL DOCUMENTS, BOOKS, and NEWSPAPERS have survived which tell us a lot about particular events.

Stories of horrible murders were especially popular. These headlines from *The Star* of 1888 were about the Jack the Ripper murders.

WHITECHAPEL

THE MURDER MANIAC SACRIFICES MORE WOMEN TO HIS THIRST FOR BLOOD.

TWO VICTIMS THIS TIME.

Many OBJECTS from the period have survived. Most of these objects are stored in museums.

Some of these old objects seem strange to us. What do you think this is? You will find the answer on page 56.

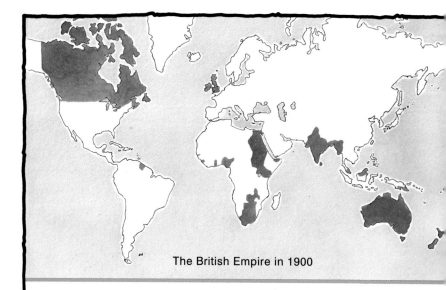
The British Empire in 1900

The legacy of the Victorians

The British Empire, which was always marked in red on maps and in atlases, stretched right round the world. It was said that 'the sun never set on the British Empire', meaning that the Empire was so big that the sun was always shining on some area ruled by Britain. The lives of millions of people were changed by British rule.

The first policemen were introduced in London in 1829. During the reigns of William IV and Victoria, other cities introduced their own police forces.

Famous organisations started in the 19th century

The Royal Society for the Prevention of Cruelty to Animals.
The National Society for the Prevention of Cruelty to Children.
The Salvation Army.

Many new inventions appeared during Queen Victoria's reign. There are far too many to show them all on this page. Here are just a few of them.

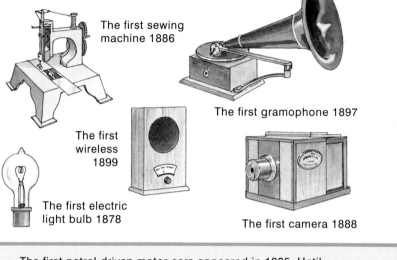

The first sewing machine 1886

The first gramophone 1897

The first wireless 1899

The first electric light bulb 1878

The first camera 1888

The first petrol-driven motor cars appeared in 1885. Until 1895 a person carrying a red flag had to walk in front of the car to keep its speed down and to warn others.

The first public lavatories were opened in London. It cost one penny to use them. This started the expression 'to spend a penny'.

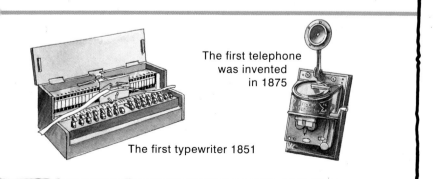

The first telephone was invented in 1875

The first typewriter 1851

Glossary

burial clubs: clubs whose members save up to pay for their own funerals

Cetewayo: pronounced Ketchewayo

charity: gifts of money and goods

compulsory: something which has to be done

dividend: a share of the profits

East India Company: a British trading company which controlled India until the 1850s

elementary education: education for young people. The Church started elementary education and still gives money to voluntary aided schools.

employees: workers

employers: business people who have employees

Gatling gun: an early type of machine gun

Industrial Revolution: a time when machines replaced people and animals as the main source of power

investment: a form of saving which makes a profit

local time: before the railways the country had many different time zones – London time was 11 minutes ahead of Bristol time. In 1852 the whole country adopted Greenwich Mean Time

missionaries: men and women who go to another country to change the religion of the people who live there

mutiny: a rebellion of soldiers against their officers

overseers: factory foremen

poor law: law about help given to poor people

privies: outside toilets. The privy was placed over a large hole in the ground. A handful of ash was thrown in after use to kill the smell

Raj: the British officials who ruled India

reformers: people who want to change things for the better

sepoys: Indian soldiers who served in the East India Company's army

suburbs: housing areas on the edge of a town

trade unions: organisations of workers who represent employees in talks with employers over rates of pay and conditions of work

Viceroy: a governor who ruled in the name of the British monarch

Index

Places to visit

Acton Scott Historic Working Farm, Shropshire
Balmoral Castle, near Ballater, Grampian region
Beamish, The North of England Open Air Museum, Durham
Brontë Parsonage Museum, Haworth, West Yorkshire
Cardiff Castle, South Glamorgan
Castell Coch, near Cardiff, South Glamorgan
Charles Dickens' Birthplace Museum, Portsmouth
Clifton Suspension Bridge, Bristol, Avon
Cotehele, St Dominick, Cornwall
David Livingstone Centre, Blantyre, Strathclyde
Dickens' House Museum, Doughty Street, London
Great Western Railway Museum, Swindon, Wiltshire
Hardy's Cottage, near Dorchester, Dorset
Hatfield House, Hertfordshire
High Level Bridge, Newcastle-upon-Tyne
Hughenden Manor, High Wycombe, Buckinghamshire
Ironbridge Gorge Museum, Telford, Shropshire
Kew Bridge Steam Museum, Brentford, Middlesex
London Transport Museum, Covent Garden Piazza, London
Michael Faraday's Laboratory and Museum,
  The Royal Institution, Albemarle Street, London
Museum of Childhood, High Street, Edinburgh
Museum of London, London Wall, London
National Army Museum, Royal Hospital Road, Chelsea, London
National Maritime Museum, Romney Road, Greenwich, London
New Lanark, near Glasgow
Osborne House, Isle of Wight
Quarry Bank Mill, Styal, Cheshire
Royal Albert Bridge, Saltash, Cornwall
Science Museum, South Kensington, London
SS *Great Britain*, Great Western Dock, Bristol, Avon
St Pancras Station, London
Victoria and Albert Museum, South Kensington, London
Victoria Square, Birmingham
Windsor Castle, Berkshire
Woburn Abbey, Bedfordshire
York Castle Museum, Eye of York, York

The object on page 51 is a carbolic acid spray. It was used
in operating theatres to squirt a fine spray of carbolic acid
over the patient to stop wounds becoming infected.